FAITH, HOPE AND CHARITY

Judith o'consent
2022
Blessings x

And now abideth faith, hope, charity, these three; but the greatest of these is charity.

1 Corinthians 13:13

King James Bible

Love is the root of missions; sacrifice is the fruit of missions

Roderick Davis

I dedicate this book to my family.

to

Andy, my strength and hopes in life's journey.

Clara and Hannah, my beautiful daughters of whom I am very proud.

Elliot William Kemp -age 9

Lucia Nicole Kemp -age 7

Poppy Jayne Kemp - age 5

My Grandchildren; -

Benjamin Thomas Ansen Michie – age 10 months

CONTENTS

Foreword

Our individual influences as a child will largely shape our future beliefs. The familiar phrase "Give me a child for her first seven years, and I'll give you the woman" - a Jesuit maxim.

Despite the debate about the actual author, its origin is five-hundred-years-old.

The renowned American Biologist, Bruce Lipton believes that a child from the years one to six is in a hypnogogic state, which means he or she absorbs everything we are told. Even the negative., for example "You are stupid and unlovable". If this is said by a significant other it will become embedded in the unconscious state, continuing to affect the way a he or she will think for the rest of their life.

Despite the difference of five hundred years, what we experience in the first seven years of life is going to affect the world as it is viewed, including how the individual feels about themselves.

If children live with criticism – They learn to condemn

If children live with hostility – They learn to fight

If children live with ridicule – They learn to be shy

If children live with shame – They learn to be guilty

If children live with encouragement – They learn confidence

If children live with tolerance – They learn to be patient

If children live with praise -They learn to appreciate

If children live with acceptance – They learn to love

If children live with approval – They learn to like themselves

If children live with honesty – They learn truthfulness

If children live with security – They learn to have faith in themselves and others

If children live with friendliness - They learn the world is a nice place in which to live.

Dorothy Law Nolte

Prologue

Missionaries are people who are called to serve God.

To serve God in a foreign country is a very humbling and dedicated profession. It always entails leaving one's abode, loved ones, one's desired life, profession and most of all one's comfortable environment. Christian Missionaries are called to serve overseas in faraway places. Countries whose climate is somewhat out of everyone's comfort zone. Not only having to live in a foreign country, they have to get accustomed to the way of life, the different culture and food.

Therefore, I owe all of my being and my gratefulness, my family, my happiness, my peace, my joy to all the missionaries I have met. I thank them for my childhood life and I thank them for being there for me, nurturing me towards my faith in God and providing me with faith in people. To be able to understand different cultures and accepting people of all denominations and status in life.

In March this year, 2021, I was 72 years old. In those 72 years, I have come a long journey and I have many people to thank along the way. I have attempted to recall those that were, have and will continue to be an influence on me. For any I have forgotten I apologise now, as that was not my intention.

Life is precious. Life is a gift. My greatest gift has been life itself as it could have been so much different.

In this book, I hope that I have been able to show my gratitude in many ways and by devoting myself to the charitable works that I have done, and will continue to do, I have been able to give back to society some of that which was given to me along the way.

Judith Townsend   2021

In the beginning

May these words of my mouth and this meditation of my heart be pleasing in your sight. Lord, my Rock and my Redeemer.

(Psalm 19:14)

Elim Mission House in Early Years

The missionaries I lived with throughout my childhood were always serving God, in villages and towns and transporting people to and from the Church.

My entire childhood life seemed to be very church based. We always had visitors from New Zealand, Australia and England to stay.

In the hall way of the home, was a round table on which there was a large visitor's book. Anyone visiting would sign and fill in a comment. I used to be fascinated by the book and often opened it to read all the comments. It must have left a big impression on me, for in my own home I keep a visitor's book on hand.

We were brought up very well, obedience was paramount to the Missionaries' agenda. Life was not a bed of roses. It was tough and regimented and we all lived by the rules and the clock. As with any family, there were good times and not so good times. Punishment was given if we crossed the line. Caning was given too if needs be.

Mrs Elizabeth Wilson was the mother figure for many years. She lived till she was 91 years old. I felt very close to her during her later years and especially at the end of life in 1967.

The compound was composed of acres of lush green fields, in which there were trees bearing tropical fruits galore. Banana trees bearing huge bunches of sweet bananas, mango trees, and rambutan trees. When the season was ready for picking, we would get a long pole and bring down the most sumptuous sweet red prickly fruit. We would indulge in them at all times.

There were star fruit trees, chigoe trees, mangosteen, papaya and pomelo trees. Fruit trees of all colours and tastes; also, a very large vegetable garden too.

We had a hen house, with hens who laid lovely eggs which we collected.

We had ducklings as well. They were bred for the table.

The gardener would attend to all these chores, pruning them and gathering in the fruits when in season. He tended to all the gardens and regularly climbed the coconut trees to bring down coconuts for our use, for baking and cooking. Unfortunately, although we savoured such great delights of tropical fruits, we had to live amongst snakes, lizards, spiders and bats galore.

The Indian gardener did a grand job cutting the lawn with a scythe. He would rise early each morning and work till noon, returning late afternoon when the heat of the day had passed.

One day, I was in rather a bad mood. The gardener had finished cutting the grass and collected it in piles ready to be removed later in the day.

Watching, I decided to mess all the piles up and run away to hide. Unfortunately, I was found out and punished very harshly.

There were huge trees surrounding the compound. I believe they were there to give shade in the very hot season, or maybe to increase the exclusivity of the compound. This thought never occurred to me at the time, but on reflection that may have been the case. We were told never to play or rest beneath the huge trees at mid-day because of the snakes and reptiles that might be on the trees.

Often, we would encounter a snake, which the gardener would assist in killing. My fear of snakes stays with me to this day and is still a big problem for me. We were taught how to catch a snake and how to avoid one, especially at noon.

The entire orphanage was massive, spanning several acres of land. We were told that to provide safety for the girls living at Elim, there were walls and gates surrounding it, encompassing the whole of the orphanage. The gates were only opened for visiting folks and the chidren going to and from school. How much of this was to reinforce the exclusivity I didn't know and only looking back could I conceive that this was indeed the case.

One of my early memories of living there would be of a very sad and lonely bearded, dirty looking individual who would live and sleep outside of the compound, under a tree at night. I could see him from my bedroom window.

He would gather sticks and light a fire every night, possibly to keep him warm during the night and fend off the many mosquitoes. The smell of the smoke still lingers in my throat.

He would collect snails, cook and eat them. He did not beg but would be asked to move on by the authorities, often. I later found out he had mental health issues.

We too, had to collect a bucket of snails each day before we went to school. We added salt to cleanse them. I think we were over run with snails.

When I think about it now, it makes me feel sick.

Elim Home

The Elim Home from its formation by Mr. and Mrs. George Wilson in 1915 had proved very popular and successful in those early years, when there was slavery or bonded servants, no free education or medical treatment.

Girls were not allowed out on their own, or to get an education or to hold jobs. After World War II the whole outlook had changed and many old ideas were thrown away.

On the political front, many countries in Asia and Africa started independence movements to fight for self-rule from the colonial powers. Slavery was outlawed and boys as well as girls enjoyed more freedom. Girls had more access to education and travel

Mr Wilson died on 6th January 1942, following a long illness in Ipoh, when the family were evacuated to Singapore and he was buried there. After the Japanese invasion, Mrs Wilson and Miss Phyllis were evacuated via India to England..

Elim Orphanage in recent times

During the Japanese occupation in Ipoh, the Church was maintained by local Elders. With the absence of the foreign missionaries, worship duty and plans were left to the local leaders and faithful senior members of the church.

Mrs. Wilson and her daughter Phyllis returned to Ipoh in October 1945 to begin the work of repairing and reorganising the "Elim Home".

Some very needy children came to the Wilsons and lived with them temporarily in the Mission House while the Girls Home, which had been turned into a 'comfort house' for immoral purposes during the Japanese occupation, was undergoing repairs and a new kitchen was being built.

When all repairs were done, the Home was reopened and some more very poor children, mostly from Christian homes were taken in.

The Social Welfare Department officer also brought in some children. It is possible that I was one of them because it was at this time that I entered the orphanage in 1949.

Having no male members of the family left, the Wilsons had to rely on local male Brethren to preach at services.

In the late 1960's, the other local Churches were able to support the poor families in their areas, so the numbers in the Elim Home decreased. When the girls were fourteen years old and home conditions were suitable, Mrs. Elizabeth Wilson and Miss Phyllis sent them home to live with their families, should they have them, and helped them with expenses, even if the families were not necessarily happy places. You see not all members of the home were orphans.

Church photo - 1950

Many girls were in the home because their Mother had died during childbirth and their Father could not cope with their upbringing. They would have annual visits from relatives to the home, in a way keeping the family connection alive. This was not available to me.

After a fall, Mrs. Wilson was weak and feeble for a few years and died on 14th January 1967 aged 91. Phyliss Wilson kept the Home going as her mother was very concerned for the remaining children even in her old age.

Early Memories

My early years in the orphanage are really vague. Maybe during certain times, I have blocked it out. We had fun collecting stones, smooth ones and playing with them or collecting match boxes to catch spiders.

We spent a lot of time on Saturday afternoons watching groups of young people coming into the compound to play rounders. We were not allowed to play instead we would spend our time playing scrabble. The game still holds dear to my heart. We started with junior scrabble and on reaching an expected level advanced to the senior game.

I got very interested in it because if we were good enough, we were allowed to stay up a bit longer at night to play with the missionary. My intention to play well meant I didn't have to go to bed so early. It was a privilege to stay up late at night.

We were taught to play the piano, having piano lessons from a teacher. It was laborious for me. I was an active child and loved the outdoors;

so, I was given a harmonica to play. I think I drove everyone mad.

We had our own bedrooms and towards the end of the closing down of the orphanage, we had plenty of rooms to choose from. The home used to cater for 100 girls at which time several girls would share a room.

The rooms were big. We had to clean our own rooms. I took pride in my bedroom, where I had a bed, a settee and a dresser. Now and again, I would move to a different room for a change of scenery. This would annoy the servants who sometimes came to clean.

We slept under mosquito nets for there were mosquitoes everywhere at night; being frightened, under the nets, made me feel safe and assured that snakes would not be able to slide into my bed.

There was also a room with a fire escape door. It was a challenge to sleep in that strange room. The door to the fire escape was never locked; almost loose. The stairs to the room never felt safe being very wobblily. The room overlooked the huge expanse of fields and trees below.

As a child, we were told stories of some of the rooms being strange or weird. I remember the main staircase being very big and wide.

There is a song which has the profound title "Nothing's Real but Love." Written and performed by the English artist Rebecca Ferguson, it conveys in just those few words a power, which instinctively strips away the beliefs and attitudes we may hold and were born with.

A new born child is enchanting but why?

It is because he or she is as yet unaffected by the world into which she or he has been delivered. An empty palette on which to paint a new life.

There are no formed views on what we may hear, see and be exposed to, being totally unaware of concepts and meanings that are taken for granted by the adult world. Concepts and meanings that shape our lives. It can be easy to extend our feelings to some people and yet to others it becomes more difficult.

Why is this?

What is it that makes some people, who are a reflection of human kind in general, more loveable than others?

Why are all people not treated the same?

In this biography I will address this conundrum. What brought an abandoned child to become a charitable institution, spreading her love and faith in whatever she applied herself too, despite a traumatic start in life?

The United Nations Convention on the Rights of the Child describes how every child has the right to an adequate standard of living to enable them to develop not only physically and mentally, but also spiritually, morally and socially. Despite this, the phenomenon of the abandoned child, seen historically in many cultures, still exists today.

How could anyone abandon a child?

There is a considerable amount of literature about child abandonment. In an impoverished society where there is high fertility, high infant mortality tends to occur. Within a shanty town, abandoned babies go undetected or unreported.

Abandonment can be viewed in many contexts but babies who are left somewhere by their parent or guardian and subsequently discovered by another person and given care and attention, or remain undiscovered and die, are considered abandoned.

Many Mothers with several children already and who abandon a child, have very strong religious beliefs and take comfort in their belief that God will care for their child.

Similarly, it is suggested that poverty and domestic violence are precursors to child abandonment and that following abandonment, mothers may become depressed and anxious through living with the guilt of deserting their child.

In many countries, cultural, religious and social stigma exists around unmarried mothers or rape victims. This possible stigma and the feeling of hopelessness in providing for a child without financial or family stability may be the main reason for mothers abandoning their babies.

In the many societies which still attach social stigma to the mothers where there is illegitimacy, rape, teenage pregnancy and poverty, consideration must be given to ways in which some potential future problems can be addressed – it is well documented that abandoned babies often suffer psychological trauma in later life if, or when, they discover they were abandoned.

Prompt discovery and access to possible medical attention, is crucial to ensure the future well-being of abandoned babies.

An abandoned baby today cannot wait for society to develop humane enlightenment. There is a need for a place which facilitates care and provides safety until such a time that the child can be placed with a caring and loving family.

It has been stated that having a name is a core element of identity. An abandoned child often has no identity or original birth date; some children may be abandoned with letters or mementos and there is a belief that these mementos may assist in the child's long-term identity and psychological development. Similarly abandoned children have no knowledge of any genetic or family medical history that may impact upon their lives.

In the 1950s, Germany initiated a baby hatch programme and many other countries have adopted this programme or provide an adaptation of it, to enable mothers or guardians to leave their babies, anonymously, in a safe place.

No such arrangements were in place in Malaysia in 1949 where I was born on the 12th March 1949 in Kuala Lumpur, or at least that is as near as anyone knows. I did not know my parents as they had abandoned me shortly after my birth. I was discovered by an unknown person who took me to hospital where I spent my first few weeks.

As I eventually became stronger it was time for me to leave and the hospital had a connection with an orphanage which was run by Missionaries, not in Kuala Lumpur, but in a town called Ipoh. This was 108 miles, 203 kilometres from the hospital. I was to be brought up there in my early years.

Missionaries in Kuala Lumpur organised the move north; they belonged to the Exclusive Brethren Church.

I was therefore on my own and moved to the orphanage in Ipoh, the Elim Orphanage. I had no family that wanted me. I had no name and didn't know who I was, where I came from or even how old I was. I had no history but I was to have a destiny, God, because to God it isn't important where you have come from but where you are going. God's destiny for the nameless, abandoned little girl was not to become a servant of a rich family, but a princess of society.

This orphanage was run by missionaries from New Zealand who belonged to the Exclusive Brethren.

The School Years

I was recognised as an intelligent child and was able to attend the Raja Perumpuan girls' school in Ipoh as my primary school. Such was my intelligence, that I had soon outstripped my fellow classmates and was being considered for elevation above my current year in the primary school.

Raja Perumpuan

girls' school, Judy four from left

To achieve this, I had to present myself for an examination. Miss Wilson, the lady with whom I had a close relationship and who had made me her favourite when I was younger, did not expect me to pass.

On getting the results, I had passed and I ran back to the home to tell the guardians. They did not believe me which destroyed my desire to continue to learn. I felt very dejected.

Nevertheless, I was to be elevated above my current year. Needless to say, to have to jump a whole year of one's school curriculum was massive and it was hard work to achieve a reasonable standard from then on.

At a later date in my life, when I was at school in Kuala Lumpur, a similar event occurred which I will recall later in the book.

We had no biological education, no sex references and more importantly for us girls, the onset of our monthly cycles.

From then on, my education went downhill. I became very stubborn and began to disobey the people running the home. As a result of our disagreement over the exam results and the mistrust that it engineered in me, I drifted apart.

My disappointment was such that it challenged my religion. I also wanted to change schools and there was one in Kuala Lumpur that attracted me, for their uniforms were green and white. Green was my favourite colour.

Bukit Bintang Girls' School (abbreviated BBGS) established in 1893 with Miss Betty Langlands teaching girls to read in Brickfields, Kuala Lumpur. Formerly known as the Chinese Girls' School, BBGS gained its name after moving to its premises on Bukit Bintang Road.

It was the oldest school in Kuala Lumpur. Sarah Shirtliff, who had come from New Zealand with Elizabeth Dron, Mrs Wilson, and who had a role in the establishment of the orphanage had been amongst the founders of this school.

Sarah Shirtliff

My memories of living with these teachers and the Missionary, were strictly controlled. I felt very awkward at school. When my classmates discovered I was living with the teachers, many ignored me as they felt I was the favourite pupil.

Mrs. Wilson
nee Elizabeth Dron

I did well in all I did at school and yet it was summarily dismissed in a way that made me think

"Why I am doing this?"

"What is the purpose of doing well, if no one accepts the results and gives me the credit for my achievement?"

I relaxed my study efforts and never tried again to impress.

To make matters worse, the Headmistress, who was a very good friend of the teachers I was living with, was a regular visitor and a church member.

I had the privilege of being amongst them at meal times, but I felt uneasy as they would discuss issues about schools. I was told to respect their privacy.

The servant would ring the breakfast gong and we would settle down to eat in silence after prayers. On completion we would all go our separate ways to school.

I was taught by all of them in the A stream but I felt I didn't fit the grade.

The missionary that was in charge of me was my Religious Knowledge teacher. I feared her because of the risk of failing any of her exams.

Eventually, we came to a cross roads, when being in charge of my Maths homework, I couldn't please her with my results.

The punishment I received was harsh. I had to stand at the bottom of her bed whilst she read a book. Unfortunately, because of all my pent-up emotions I misbehaved very mischievously.

One day, whilst she was reading the Daily Telegraph newspaper, I carefully crawled up towards her and punched a hole in the centre of the paper.

My punishment for that was even more harsh. I was made to stand, in bare feet, on the hottest side of the house from noon for several hours. I remember my feet being burnt, despite an attempt to relieve the pain by alternating the foot I was standing on.

I often cried myself to sleep, I felt unwanted and didn't really understand the reason for the punishment.

I stayed with her until one evening that I had a lot of Maths problems to solve. Mathematics was not my favourite subject but it was passable.

I had been given a lot of homework to do by the Missionary. There were some problems I couldn't solve in the allotted time.

It was getting late and my brain was exhausted. I was weary from the tasks in hand. She came to check on my progress. When she opened the door to find me still struggling with the algebra, I had my knuckles smacked and was told to think and use my brains.

Tears were rolling down my cheeks and I was left to complete the page.

I sat and sobbed my heart out. I wanted to go to bed. Only when an English teacher, who was staying with us, opened the door could I then get out of the room in which I had been locked.

She asked why I was so upset. I related the problem to her to which she said

'Go to bed'.

A huge argument followed as to why I had not completed the maths problems. This wasn't good enough for the missionary.

I went and within minutes there was an almighty row. I felt responsible for getting that teacher into trouble. Things got worse for the following morning at breakfast, the mood was very severe with an icy atmosphere. The remarks I overheard were

'Do not interfere, I am in charge of Judy.'

When I was taken to school the next day, I went in search of this lovely teacher to apologise to her. Unfortunately, she left and found an alternative place to live.

I became increasingly unhappy at school, having to live with the teachers who taught me. To be the ideal pupil and the expectation for me to reach the highest potential, was making me really anxious.

To end it all, the final treatment I received, was to be sent back to Ipoh to be with Miss Phyliss Wilson. I got in touch with her and she came to collect me.

To this day, those unhappy memories are still embedded in my mind whenever I think of Kuala Lumpur and Bukit Bintang Girls Secondary school.

Maybe they had realised that they could not contain my rebellious character. My schooling was continued from then on at a co-educational school and a sixth form, at the Methodist English School, Ipoh, with somewhat of a great relief.

The Methodist English School, Ipoh, was a government secondary school located Jalan Raja Ashman Shah, Ipoh, Perak. This school was an English school established during British occupation in Malaya. The school had been established since 1909.

This was a co-educational school. I was able to prove to everyone that I was good enough for I was made the Head Senior prefect of the year on selection by the teachers.

It was to be the happiest time of my childhood. I was able to excel in sports and arts. As a teenager, I felt a freedom at last, after years of being hemmed in by the Missionaries and teachers who insisted that I became the perfect pupil, who had to aim to my very best at school.

At a year group challenge, we were given a task to design a pattern for the Batik Company, who made clothes. The best design would be presented to the company to be printed.

I was very eager to put my pattern into action. I drew several designs and finally presented the one I was happy with; my final piece. All entries were sent off to be examined and to my delight, it was

Judy second left.

announced at school assembly that mine had been chosen.

I was awarded a book token as a prize. It felt good to be proven that I could achieve something at last.

I had always felt that I was not clever enough, not good enough, I could do much better. It made me feel such a failure and a disappointment to those in charge of me.

The other achievement was my ability to join the school athletic team.

Being able to run and enjoy being outside, I joined the team. I was allowed to play all sports; badminton, table tennis and swimming were my favourite past times.

I believe I was allowed to take up these activities, as the Missionaries thought this would calm my attitude towards them.

I excelled in most sports, winning many trophies over time, on track events. I joined the mixed relay team for field competitions. Many shields were won. Sports master on the right and my fellow running companions.

I was given a bike so that I could take myself to school and all these after school events.

I remember spending many afternoons and Saturdays on the track practising so that I could better myself. Often it was impossible as the heat of the day would sap my energy.

However, I did become an accomplished athlete in all sprint, track events – 100,200 and 400 metres – with relays included.

I was good enough to represent my county in the inter-school championships, but this was contrary to Brethren beliefs in engaging in sporting activities on Sundays. At the time I was given no explanation for this.

Why I was allowed to do it, I do not know. There were restrictions!

The competition into which I was entered was the South-East Asia games and it was to be held over three days to allow for heats and finals. It was on a Friday, Saturday and Sunday.

Sunday!

Once Miss Wilson discovered that I would be away from services on that Sunday, they stopped me competing. Yet another fuel to my internal stress. They told me to ask the team to find another competitor to take my place.

I had to attend church. The most memorable time in this time of my life is when I attended a Christian Conference organised by Billy Graham, the well-known World Evangelist. He was supposed to arrive in Malaysia to preach the word of God to the local inhabitants. However, as Malayia was and is a Muslim country, he was not allowed to come. His second in command, Grady Wilson came in his stead.

Girls Bible School

Several conferences were held throughout Asia with one in particular at the Gospel Hall in Ipoh, which I was able to attend.

It was the missionaries abiding wish that all girls from the orphanage would attend a full week of daily sermons.

It was also their desire that we would dedicate our lives to Christ.

The nightly sermons we attended were very earnest, powerful and appealing. I listened, as I did in each of the three or four services, I attended each Sunday. You get accustomed to the calling and way they preach and plead people to come forward for acceptance.

During one of the few final days of the intense preaching, I felt a voice calling me to open my hearts' door.

In accepting Christ as my saviour and Lord, I felt an over whelming glow of love, peace and joy. Going forward to the front, I knelt down and gave my life to Christ.

When returning home from the service, I knelt and prayed to thank God for showing me his wonderful love and grace.

When I was fourteen years old, I was baptised by full immersion. It was a day I shall never forget for to this day, God has truly been my protector, my guardian angel, my hopes and joys.

Whenever I falter, He upholds me. He never lets me down. He lifts me up when I fall.

Our God is a great God.

ELIZABETH WILSON

Mrs Elizabeth Wilson was my mother figure for many years. She lived till 91 years old. I felt very close to her during her and towards the end of her life, in 1967.

Mrs Wilson and me 1949

I believe I was told I was her favourite. We would spend a lot of evenings together, taking evening walks as the sun was setting.

We would walk to the very end of the compound, surrounded by walled fences and gates. She would walk with a stick and I would hold her hand.

Along the way, she would engage me in stories from the bible, encouraging me to become a Christian. I feel now that it was her dearest wish.

When we arrived at the bottom of the field, there would be a huge bonfire, piled up with rubbish, coconut husks and a variety of flammable waste.

There we would watch the flames go up and I clearly remember that she would love to poke and push it with her stick.

I enjoyed those walks and the closeness with her. I regret now not understanding her more. I should have asked more questions regarding who I was and why was I living in the orphanage?

She had lived with us on one side of the compound. Then there was the Church, next a very big building which was used basically for visitors, visiting missionaries. There were other houses down there on the other side of the compound.

I remember Mrs. Elizabeth Wilson living in the third one. Because I was close to her and much more so towards a time in her later years. She wanted me to be there or I decided that she required more attention. I went to look after her and I would sleep with her at night whilst Miss Wilson would go back to the orphanage and look after the other girls.

I was the one she needed because she had a lot of vivid dreams. She would always fall in them. And if she fell, she would call out and shout and then nobody would go but me.

I would go and pick her up usually bruised or cut. I remember one time she fell; it was a Sunday and she was badly bruised. I couldn't pick her up. She was getting quite old and heavy and I had to call the other girls to come and give me help. I needed help to lift her out and take her back home.

It was from that day that she began her deterioration and I decided I wanted stay with her to keep watch. I slept on the next bed with her, just to look after her and make sure she didn't fall at night.

I didn't feel happy there because unfortunately I have got a bad phobia of snakes. There were snakes everywhere where we lived and I saw one climb up one day along the window.

I said to Mrs Wilson

"I don't like this. I don't like you being here alone."

In view of my comments and worries, in the end we all moved back into the orphanage. It was towards the end of her life.

My fears were realised when I was having a bad day, possibly playing on my own, on a very hot sultry day.

I decided to return to the mission house to see if I could get an answer to my troubled thoughts and fears.

"To whom did I belong?"

"Why was I living with other girls in an orphanage?"

I knocked on the office door, approaching Miss Phyliss Wilson who was there, with fear in my heart. I did not get a valid response to my questions but was fobbed off with a bar of Cadbury's nut chocolate. A rare sight indeed. Being told to eat it, I sat outside eating it. but it did not fill the void I still felt inside.

The only medical treatment we received on a regular basis was designed to stop us getting coughs and colds. A boiler was heated by a wood fire outside in the compound, and towels placed in the hot water. We were stripped off and rubbed all over with olive oil and a very hot towel wrapped around us. This event was a monthly tradition. How it was supposed to work, I do not know, but to this day it is rare for me to get caught with a cold or cough.

Death of

Mrs Elizabeth Wilson

The Lord lifts up his [approving] countenance upon me and gives me peace (Numbers 6:26)

After a fall, Mrs. Wilson was weak and feeble for a few years and died on 14th January 1967 aged 91.

Before she died, she had been honoured by the Government for all her work over the years. Her funeral, which I remember clearly, was like the funeral fit for dignitaries.

When she was very ill, before her death, I would spend a lot of time with her; I suppose I looked on her as my Granny. She would ask me to read from the Bible, in particular Psalms, and she would correct me if I got them wrong.

One day when the doctors had left, she asked me to open the cupboard which was situated opposite the foot of her bed. Inside was a large wooden box which she asked me to bring to her. Inside was a white gown, covered in Lace décor. She asked me to make sure that when she died, she would be dressed in this for the funeral.

Towards the end of her life. I was called by Phyliss to sit beside her. Her wish was for me to read slowly and not recite the whole chapter which I knew, to Mrs Wilson.

Whilst I was reading, the Lord took her to be with Him.   Since then, I have never been afraid of death.   As young children, we taught about Death, Heaven and Hell.

I remember Phyliss telling me she looked so peaceful.   Every wrinkle had disappeared from her face.   The doctor was called to certify the passing.

She died of pneumonia if I remember correctly, whereupon Miss Phyllis asked me to help her prepare the body for the funeral.   I accepted the invitation and was not worried by the presence of the body.

We washed her and put on this beautiful gown that she had shown me. There was a beautiful and peaceful atmosphere.

The preparation of her burial went ahead and a lot of dignities and missionaries came to pay their respects.

She had been placed in an open coffin so that many of the Brethren could pay their respects before she was buried. I stood alongside the coffin without fear. The handling of the body and its preparation was yet again pushing my ambition to be a nurse. I was able to be there to unveil the coffin for viewing.

Malaya is a very hot country so you can imagine a body could decompose rapidly. To prevent this, we placed the body in a wooden box and packed ice, large blocks, around it to keep it cool.

She had died on the 14th January 1967.

It was a very big funeral. The procession was manned by a police escort along the way to the cemetery. I remember marching, we had to march along the streets and the roads were all closed for her. We were given sweets to eat.

It was the end of an era. A faithful servant of God, laid to rest in a foreign country.

It must have been all the emotions and activities of those final days that reinforced my desire to be a nurse.

Deep down I thought a lot of Elizabeth Wilson and was told I was her favourite baby.

I thank God for both of the Wilsons for nurturing and guiding me throughout my life. I ask for forgiveness for not conforming and often being so disobedient, I am sure this caused them pain.

Phyliss Wilson and me in the middle

Life is a mystery. It is often not until we lose someone dear to us, that we have these many regrets.

We cannot turn back the clock. But we can try and fulfil all the wondrous works that have been passed to us and make them work now.

I have many people to thank and for those past and present, I am eternally grateful for every effort and care that has been and is shown to me.

As the economic situation improved and advanced in the late1960's, the other local Churches were able to support the poor families in their areas, so the numbers in the Elim Home decreased. four us that remained; Christine, Grace, Wendy and me.

When the girls were old enough and home conditions were suitable, the children were sent home to live with their families, should they have them, and helped them with expenses, even if the families were not necessarily happy places. You see not all members of the home were orphans.

Grace, me, and Christine, Wendy in the middle

Many girls were in the home because their Mother had died during childbirth and their Father could not cope with their upbringing. They would have annual visits from relatives to the home, in a way keeping the family connection alive.

It was the same with the boys. In this way those children grew in a 'family' environment. The remaining children, those that had them, were progressively channelled back to their families. I had none of this available to me.

Toki Myashina's version of the 23rd psalm

The Lord is my pace-setter, I shall not rush.
He makes me stop and rest for quiet intervals.
He provides me with images of stillness
which restores my serenity.

He leaves me ways of efficiency through
calmness of mind, and his guidance is peace.
Even though I have a great many things
to accomplish each day, I will not fret,
for his presence is there.

His timelessness, his all importance

will keep me in balance.
He prepares refreshment and renewal
in the midst of activity.

By anointing my mind with His oils
of tranquillity, my cup of joyous
energy overflows.

Surely harmony and effectiveness
shall be fruits of my hours,
for I shall walk in the peace of the
Lord,
and dwell in his house for ever.

Toki Myashina -
Psalm 23 will always hold dear to my
heart.

Nurse

When I was nine years old, I was
taken ill and admitted to hospital.
When any of the children became
unwell, we would be told to go to bed

with a glass of water. Other complaints were often dismissed.

For several days I had an acute stomach pain on my right side. All I was told was 'go to the toilet'.

The pain became worse and on one occasion I decided to go down the stairs to ask for help. In so much severe pain, I staggered out of the bedroom and fell down the stair well and collapsed thereafter.

Fortunately, someone heard my cry and came to my aid. I was rushed to hospital and immediately to theatre; there it was discovered that I had a ruptured appendix and in a close call for a severe peritonitis which could have been fatal.

However, waking up in the hospital, I looked up and there were bright lights overhead. I thought I was in heaven, but this must have been the theatre in which my appendix was removed. I had no recollection of how I had got there or why.

I was transferred to a hospital ward. It was an awful place. Not very clean with cats roaming throughout the wards. It was very hot; no air conditioning and it was clear that I was not expected to live because my bed was between a dying old lady and a seriously ill child.

Despite the state of the institution, the attendance and care I received was completely new to me. The care given me by a particular nurse was very basic, but it was such a new experience to me. Looking back, it was to trigger my desire to be a nurse.

As my health improved, I was allowed to help that nurse, in her office, to roll up cotton into balls for dressings. I felt useful in doing that and from then on, nursing was my ambition; I wanted to become a nurse. I was nine years old.

The life I had led up to this point was to be in line with Bruce Lipton's hypothesis that children in the first seven years of their life are hypnogogic, sponge like in that they absorb everything. This absorption shapes their future beliefs and actions.

For me that environment gave me my faith, the recognition of care in the community, discipline and a work ethic that had to be 110%. The Faith, Hope and Charity that I have practised throughout my life and which is the driver behind this biography.

I have wanted to share these qualities with those to whom I speak, serve and hopefully inspire. Given the right direction, even from the lowly start in life that I had, you can achieve your ambition.

Discipline

I need to make the point that I am grateful for what the Missionaries did for me. In coming to the orphanage and in my early childhood life was very difficult for me.

I proved to be a very difficult child. I could be very challenging; difficult to handle.

Maybe I was difficult because I didn't know who I was. I never felt loved. I felt that I was just a number.

During our childhood days in the orphanage, we had a servant to look after us. She was not a decent lady; full of nastiness. She used to pour water over our heads and spank us for whatever reason she felt was necessary. She would feed us till we couldn't take anymore and then force food down our throats.

Very often the Missionary would sit us down with extra homework. It was not a fun thing but a test of mental arithmetic. If anyone of us there, got only one of the sums wrong and we would get smacked, I would be the one that would giggle. I don't know what made me do that. I would giggle and I would get slapped on my hands for giggling and this brought me nothing good, just grief.

Today, you're not allowed to touch any children. You know not to smack anybody but I don't think they did it then without thought. I didn't think it was that bad of a thing for me to laugh or giggle.

That's discipline without question, but was it their individual decision to do that, or was it a directive they had from the Church.

I like to believe it was because they wanted us to do well; they wanted us to progress and they wanted us to meet a target. They thought we should behave in a determined manner and therefore this little act of being silly was wrong. They had to be firm with us.

In the past and with the girls who shared that life with me, I have asked

"Were we ever loved?"

I know now and I think I remember not being loved. It was almost a sense of being in a military position. If I could describe it that way, it was as though you had no individual personal close contact. No recognised individuality. I can't remember if I had that, but maybe I did when I was little.

When I was growing up. I felt we were just on our own. You had to survive, by going to school, doing our work and maybe spend some fun time on Saturday.

You might have a little free space then. Time to play outside but there was almost no emotional contact. I can't remember them giving any of us that contact. So maybe the Missionaries had no other idea how they would motivate us or how they would plan and mould our future. I don't know if that was true, but I felt that way, anyway, looking back.

Today, if I was asked to choose any aspect of a great role model, I think it would be the missionary aspect that has formed part of and continued through my life. Lots of the missionaries came from Australia, New Zealand and I met them. I saw a different sort of side to them.

I admired them, you know in a way, for what they gave up, crossing oceans and their sacrifices to those in need. I was moved by this, for they literally gave a lot of their lives, maybe a hundred percent of their lives to go wherever they were sent. To proclaim the gospel to help the sick and the lonely and the orphans so there must have been something very special in these missionaries.

There were times looking back, when I thought I'd like to be a missionary; but then I thought, why am I thinking about this when I have forwarded my life in England and now, I don't need to go abroad to be missionary. I am a complete missionary where I am; in the community.

Lonely

Once a year, the orphanage was open to visitors, relatives and children. At the given time, I would lock myself in my room.

Throughout that day, other children would be taken out to see their families, accepting gifts brought for them by their folks.

It was not a good day for me as I knew no one would come to see me. I would wait for the visitors to leave when I could go and ask if any of the others would share some of their parcels with me. It did not happen which really upset me. At this time, my dislike for the other girls was enormous. I remember pinching a banana from a bowl and was caught doing this, only to receive punishment for my act.

Holidays

Once a year we would be taken to the highlands where the air would be much cooler and fresher.

As children we loved these holidays up the very steep, winding and rocky roads to the Cameron Highlands.

It meant we could have fun and no tuition classes. We stayed at this beautiful cool accommodation where there was a Butler, who provided our meals.

We were given instructions when we arrived never to leave the premises. On one occasion, I got up very early to breath the fresh air and green, green grass below my room.

There was a bench where I sat to watch the golfers teeing off. Suddenly, I heard a loud bark and roar. I was frozen with fright.

An Alsatian dog was running towards me. I ran and screamed so loud. Fortunately, the Butler heard my cry and took command of the dog, getting it to stay.

He took me in and I received the loudest lecture from all corners. Never did I realise that it was a vicious guard dog and I was lucky to be alive. I fear dogs to this day.

The only other holidays we went on were at the church Bible Resort in Penang.

The Brethren Church owns a huge complex hotel on the beach in Batu Ferrengi Literally. We would be put on a train in Ipoh and collected by Elders at the other end.

I really enjoyed the train journey to and fro but not the routine of the day to day running of the conference.

It's called Christian convention holiday. You stay in dormitories, living and breathing the Bible. It's quite bizarre thinking about it. The word holiday was basically a misnomer because you were working all the time.

Looking back, it was a week of teaching, supporting and befriending older Christians. Praying, reading and worship were paramount to each day's agenda.

Towards the end of the week, it was testimony time for those who gave their live to Christ.

It reminded me of being back at school. My thoughts and mind would wander, floating around wishing all these lectures would soon be over. I wanted to go and swim in the warm sea.

I loved the sound of the waves crashing against my feet and toes on the hot, white sand. All good things came to an end and we were taken back to the home.

Maybe the hope was, that we accepted, believed and upheld the Christian Faith in our lives.

I am sure a lot of truths would have been instilled in me but at that time I was not ready for full conversion.

You would have breakfast, go for Bible study and never have an hour to rest. People were there for Bible study at night. We had to go every year to this conference and prayer times.

That's why my Husband can tell you that I hate the hustle of holidays because it reminds me of being told what to observe and obey, do everything as they say. I wasn't going to the beach and having a relaxation or fun times.

It was just controlled, and this is how I felt our holidays were.

I'm very happy at home. I love my home and I have no intention of leaving. I feel that flying in an aeroplane, being in an airport wasting those hours queuing up and sitting around just depresses me.

I've been back 3 times I've been back to see the orphanage; and all my friends.

Labrooy

When Mrs Elizabeth Wilson died, Miss Phyllis decided to take a sabbatical.

As the orphanage was closing down. There were only two of us left behind, Christine and myself.

She had a very good friend, who I think was a millionaire in Malaysia, who supported the mission. There is a clear memory of this lady, for we went to stay with her.

Her name was Leila Allanah Labrooy. It was her house that we went to at Christmas.

The LaBrooys, though relatively new to Ipoh at that time, had built considerable wealth and influence, especially in construction and real estate.

They could trace their ancestry to the Dutch Burghers in Ceylon (Sri Lanka), descended from the intermarriage between Dutch colonists and local women. Most prominent among the Ipoh LaBrooys is a certain Claude Henry LaBrooy, who was an architect and contractor.

He was responsible for the early construction of the mission house in which I spent my childhood. He built the whole village that's where she, Leila, got her money from, for he was the architect. She never told us anything about them. We never knew anything about them. He built the original mission, where I lived, in 1913. I was quite surprised when I was told this in the research for this book.

The Mission House was made of half-wood, half-concrete. Building work started in 1913 most probably before the Wilsons went on leave and the building was completed in early 1914. A baptism pool made of cement was built beside the house for baptism services.

The Mission House - build in 1913

Around this time the first assembly conference was held in Ipoh. As the Mission House was not quite ready for use, the conference was held in a workers' construction shed in the Labrooy compound in Dulcieville Lane, behind the Main Convent School.

Leila Allanah Labrooy, was a very dedicated Christian, very solid in her beliefs. Our real Mother Teresa and we were sent to live with her. She must have inherited money from her father's business. That's why she was able to have all the chidren there for Christmas and us last two girls to stay whilst Miss Phyllis was away.

At first, we were quite scared because she was very serious and very noted in the Brethren Church. She was a church organist as well. She was very strict in her whole appearance.

When we were told that Miss Wilson was going on the sabbatical, Christine and I had the privilege of staying with her whilst Miss Wilson was away.

When at first, we were told we were going to live with Aunty Leila, we were shocked and terrified because she looked very serious.

CLAUDE LABROOY

We knew where she lived as our Christmas parties were always in her vast gardens full of various tropical fruit trees, especially large mangoes.

As children, when we were taken there for high teas. We were always dressed beautifully. Best polished shoes, best frocks and neatly tided hair.

We were taught good table manners. The table was loaded with succulent sandwiches and cakes. I still remember today the cucumber sandwiches, which I still enjoy today.

When we were sent there, we wondered at the size of the house?

She lived in a large bleak Plantation house. She owned several houses there along the drive, which were lived in by her relatives.

She would give her life, her time and her money in helping the poor and needy. To us she gave an insight into how a Christian should live,

It was quite an awesome place; we had strict rules to follow whilst staying there. We were not allowed out of the house because she had very many big Alsatians that were vicious. They would roam free in the grounds as security because the crime levels in that area were very high.

The whole house was run by cooks and servants. When we arrived, we were shown our bedroom and this enormous the living room; it would sit about 20 people easily and had a big grand piano.

We were shown our bedroom with an en-suite bathroom. Two beautiful single beds with white ironed sheets. A large dressing table and chairs for our comfort. It was beyond our imagination.

The most fascinating thing about living there, was the routine which we had to observe. She told us that in the morning when we get up, there will be a dong. A strike on a gong in the hallway. We were given an explanation of what these dongs were about.

The gong was struck by the head man, a butler in many ways. He was always on call for her. He wore a completely white robe and a white serviette on his arm but he was on call for her need, day and night.

He was the person responsible for sounding the commands on the gong. He would be the one that would hit the first dong. This was in place of a call or a shout that would tell us to be ready for your breakfast. Are you ready for your lunch? Are you ready for your dinner?

The second dong was sounded when you had better be ready and coming down to the dining room. We had to be dressed for the occasion. At our first attempt, we made our first mistake. We entered the dining room and made to go and sit down. We were told off completely. We had to stand up and stand behind the chair. Standing there, we had to wait patiently. We didn't know what it was all about. But we had to get up put the chair back in.

We had to wait until Miss Labrooy came down. She was accompanied by a man with her as well. It was either her nephew or her brother-in-law, we never found out for sure, but he too would come down.

We all stood up and waited until she arrived, at which point the butler, would pull the chair out for her. Letting her sit down, he would then get a serviette and put it on her lap.

We had to watch all that, as it was repeated as he came to others at the table; then came to us to do the same. It was huge learning curve for us. It was there to be observed, to show us that's how we should live. It was quite fascinating compared to how we were living in the orphanage, where we had to get ourselves up, get breakfast and get everything else during the day.

Once seated, the butler would place a beautifully ironed serviette on our knees. This was repeated for every meal

What fascinated me in this huge big banqueting-hall, was a big sideboard at the end of the room. On there was not just one main meal, there were several, I would say four or five main meals. They were set in huge big silver like caldrons.

There was a choice, of all this new to us. I remember thinking is this really just for the four of us.

"Who's going to eat all that food?"

Not thinking anything other than we had a choice. We chose what we wanted and I will not forget that first meal with them. I was so sick afterwards because it was such rich food, a complete contrast to how we ate in the orphanage. We had to slow down because we realised, we couldn't do that, over eat, for there were puddings as well. It troubled me because I didn't realise what an earth was this all about.

"What happened to all the left-over food?"

It was a huge culture shock really. It was beyond anything we had seen before. It troubled my mind as to how somebody could be so different from where we came from; from what we had!

In the orphanage we were well fed, but this was just like food maybe fit for the Queen, it was just amazing. It was a very lovely place and we felt very honoured to be there; I could have easily imagined that I was in a palace.

My inquisitive mind started to work again. We weren't supposed to talk to the servants; we had to accept that.

However, I wanted to talk to them and one day I went down from my room in the afternoon, for I had waited till Miss Labrooy went to sleep. I went down the servant's quarters and asked the maid,

"Can you tell me what happens to all that food?"

She said,

"The servants would have it first, then it would be a cleaner who helped, the laundry lady, and the gardener. They would eat what they wanted but after that it all went to the street people".

Often, Miss Labrooy would give all the left-over food to the convent for the nuns. Wasn't that wonderful? Nobody would have known that, except, because we lived there, we knew.

Every Christmas, as children, we went to her house. We did have Christmas morning at our house in the orphanage but afterwards, we went to her house. That's how we knew her from very young and this guy who was quite a large man, the brother-in-law, would dress up as Santa. We all had to sit on his knee to get a present. I just didn't like his red clothes and I didn't like his beard. I refused and I would be the last one to go get my present because I wouldn't sit on his knee and I would just take it off him.

Every Christmas, she would set out a beautiful long table for all the children and we would go there and have a good Christmas party. I did go and see her before she died. She was lovely.

Leila Labrooy. What a wonderful woman, a saint and a legend in many ways. A true Christian Lady, living the true Christian faith.

We were so grateful for the time that we were able to live with her. A Lady whom I respected and who, like Jesus, met with people of all races, colour or creed.

She met with the beggars, the poor and needy. She fed millions unknown to many people. She gave much to charity and when she passed after a short illness, the Authorities recognised her. She was just amazing and when she died apparently a lot of the roads were named after her which I saw when I went back.

We lived there for a year while Miss Phyllis was away, for she did not return until December 1968, having left in the January. Miss Labrooy took us to school each day.

Phyliss Wilson

It was shortly after the death of her mother that she went back to New Zealand. That's when Christine and I had to go and live with Miss Labrooy, for a period of a year before Phyllis Wilson came back.

She left after her mother's funeral which was in January 1967, and she came back in the December.

Phyllis had sacrificed leading a normal life, perhaps the possibility of a marriage and aspirations to become a doctor, to bring us up because of her loyalty to her parents, Faith and God. Her love for God convinced her to walk in obedience to her calling. She assumed the role of a single mother which could not have been easy let alone to care and be responsible for emotionally insecure children who were not her own.

I truly now respect and honour her brave and diligence that she led for us.

I am one of the living proofs of her love and commitment to orphans like me who needed the care and guidance to grow and become fulfilled individuals.

Miss Wilson always drove a car and if we were good children, our treat on a Saturday, would be a car ride to an aerodrome in Ipoh, to watch the planes fly in and depart.

I remember clearly the exciting thoughts of how lovely it would be if one day I could be on a plane, flying to a far away country and never return to the home.

My dreams did eventually come true.

Final Occupation

By this time the orphanage was nearly empty and only four girls remained, Christine, Wendy, Grace and me. Eventually there was just me and I lived with Miss Phyllis.

I don't want to be too harsh on the Missionaries. For them to come from a foreign country, maybe at the call of God, to teach and spread the Gospel was a sacrifice to their beliefs. I feel that they sacrificed human emotion to the dedication of the job. The job in the Christian Faith. It had its very good side, for instance the help they gave to communities.

Johore Bahru is the capital of the state of Johore, Malaysia. It is situated along the Straits of Johore at the southern end of Peninsular Malaysia, opposite the independent country of Singapore. Miss Phyllis and I travelled the 500 kilometres there, from Ipoh, in 1970.

Miss Phyllis drove a car. I don't remember how long it took to cover the distance but we must have stopped somewhere along the way.

We had used this car frequently and in the height of summer would travel up into the hills, the Cameron Highlands, to cool off. As children, we loved these holiday trips to the family holiday house of the Labrooy's, as it meant no tuition classes.

I remember the roads to the Highlands being very bad and tortuous, but Miss Phyllis was a good driver. I was still terrified though by each and every journey.

To develop the new Gospel Hall, Miss Phyllis could not have done that on her own, as the Brethren discipline requires male Elders to take services. I assume that there must have been a Brethren community already established in Johore before our arrival. I do know that Miss Phyllis played the organ at each service. The Gospel Hall in Ipoh Bahru was much bigger than the Hall in Johore.

I know in later years when she stayed with me, she had problems with her health. I couldn't figure it out why then, but maybe as a nurse and getting older and wiser it has become clear.

It could be she was calling for help towards the end. She wanted me to know and now it makes sense. She talked about bleeding inside and I remember thinking is it because she's suffering from stress and anxiety? She should have told us about what's happening. She could have told us why she moved to Johore.

I feel very sad for her in view of what she had done for me; for what she had given up to spend so much time with her Mother. It was a great pity that she had to come to an end like that.

She was a bit too liberal possibly. She was very lenient towards us at the end as we grew older, to towards me anyway, and she still had to have that control over us.

She was in Johore Bahru from 1968 to 1980. In retirement she went back to New Zealand where she died in 2002. She lived with no money. She had to open her house to guests to survive.

There was no one who would support her in New Zealand where she was retired to. I wondered how she would have an income. We heard that she opened her house to the Chinese pupils of Chinese parents so that she could earn some money. The Chinese students literally cheated on her and didn't pay her and she died with no money. I often wonder how she progressed from being involved with her Mother in Ipoh and then gradually being moved out. I didn't know why or how the Church could do that.

In my life before leaving, had I seen Phyliss as a role model to follow. I left her obviously, not in a very good situation. I was very upset. All through growing up with her, she was our guardian.

I don't know what influence she had on me, in the context of the Church. We, as women, were not allowed to speak during the service. She would be the one that took care in the moulding of my Christianity, moulded my faith in right the way of that Brethren Church. We were taught that in Sunday school.

If I were to identify with anyone in that position of a role model for me, I would choose "Mother Teresa". She was a missionary, a nurse and a saviour of children and it has been my life works to follow a similar pattern. Her faith was strong and I hope mine has been the same.

It must be a calling from God to become a missionary. She looked after us, Phyllis Wilson, but her mission came to the end with that flight back in 1980, to live in New Zealand.

She did come and stay with me and my husband in later years. It was the first time she opened up to me and said that she only went to Malaysia to join her mother who was a missionary. She actually was a very talented lady, for she gave up her life to be with her Mother in the orphanage and to heal the sick and wounded in poor villages.

She sacrificed her ambition to be a doctor for at the end she was a very lonely lady.

Johore Bahru

Miss Phyllis Wilson served in Johore Bahru from 1968-1980. In 1980 she made a visit to Ipoh to Elim Gospel Hall for a reunion with old friends before she retired to New Zealand due to health reasons. She died in New Zealand in December 2002 in poverty.

During her last years she became more charismatic, showing a compelling charm which inspired devotion in others. but still maintained the strict discipline of the Brethren Church.

I lived with her in Johore Bahru for two years until 1970. During that time, I had begun seeking jobs and had placed advertisements in the nearby Naval Base for a position as an Amah, a family servant.

I became friendly with the daughter of a Brethren family who attended the Gospel Hall in Johore. She was in my Sunday Bible class. She lived across the road from the Gospel Hall. Her family were more outgoing and Nicola, their daughter became a close friend. I was allowed to visit them and spend time with Nicola.

As a small child I used to have horrible dreams where grotesque characters would appear and frighten me. It was on one visit to the local town with my new family friend, that

I saw Chinese Opera for the first time. There, on stage, were the grotesque characters of my early dreams!

It was not until a certain Sunday that I was faced with a dilemma. I disobeyed by going out with Nicola, who lived opposite our Church.

We went out this time with permission to town, but the instructions were that I had to be back home to deal with the preparation of the Church before the congregation arrived Coming back to the Johore home from this Chinese Opera, I was late and the gates to the missionary house were closed. Miss Phyllis Wilson was on the inside, she had been waiting, counting down my absence.

My lateness was a step too far!

Judy age sixteen

.

She had kindly given me an allowance to go to the show on the condition, clearly laid down, that I could go, as long as I was back in time for evening service. I had broken that agreement and without question, she gave me 20 minutes to pack and leave.

After Miss Wilson put me out on the street with just my clothes and no money. I was walking away wondering what to do and I went to Nicola's house. Her Mother invited me to come and live with them and it was through this family that I got my position as an Amah looking after a disabled child, which I was to hold for a few months.

I needed a permanent job as I was keen to come to England and start my nursing career. I put a notice in the NAAFI at the Naval base, offering my services as an Amah. In a few days through that, I got the job with the Tunstall family; the Husband was a Naval Officer.

It was important to me that I should become self-supporting after the break up with Miss Wilson. I was able to continue as an Amah after the Tunstalls left for England when I joined the Dann family, another Naval officer, until I left for England in 1972.

After being excluded by Miss Phyllis, I left the Brethren Church but not my faith, joining the local Church of England on the Naval base. I attended each Sunday, walking to it.

My jobs as an Amah came to an end with the return to England of the Naval Officers for whose family I had worked. I did however keep in touch with the Dann family from Portsmouth.

I sent applications to various hospitals in England.- All the hospitals replied and all of them offered me a position but I chose to accept the response from Huddersfield, as going there in a foreign country, I would have connections with the Tunstall family who lived close by.

I had often expressed my ambition to the Tunstall family, who offered to sponsor me to emigrate to England to study nursing. All I had to do was to save sufficient money to buy my air ticket and they would do the rest.

Since the 1962 Commonwealth Immigrants Act by the United Kingdom Parliament, restrictions were placed on immigration from current and former British colonies, and these were tightened by successive governments. The Immigration act included a voucher system and significant Chinese migration to Britain did still continue by relatives of already settled Chinese and by those qualified for skilled jobs, until the end of the 1970s.

By 1972, only holders of work permits, or people with parents or grandparents born in the UK could gain entry – significantly reducing primary immigration from Commonwealth countries. I had to apply for my work permit. In this I was aided by both the Dann and Tunstall families.

Freedom

After years of living under very strict rules, I felt I needed to be free. Free to search for myself and begin to know who I was.

To be able to think for myself, have some self esteem and get back control of my own well-being. Not to be told to do this and do that.

I wanted to climb to higher grounds. I needed to be away to another country. There was no one here for me in Malaysia. No one to understand my pain, my hopes and my ambition.

Although I stayed with Phyliss for a couple of years in Johore Bahru, I felt aimless and unfulfilled. I helped in Church Services and Sunday school but the rest of the week was very unproductive.

Andy

One day on my way home from the Naval base, I passed a Church where from within I could hear music, guitars and singing. Back in Ipoh in the Gospel Hall we included music in our services with guitars and piano, on which I was taught. The sounds coming from this Church made me think that this was an Evangelical Pentecostal Church and I was curious.

As I stood there listening, a sailor splendid in his tropical whites (I always had a thing for uniforms), stopped and asked if he could help. He explained that this was an Evangelical Church and he was part of the congregation where he played the guitar during services.

He spent his Sundays in observance and unlike other sailors who drank and smoked, he didn't; his name was Ansen Townsend.

I began to attend on occasional Sundays at this Church and Andy and I became friends. But I preferred the Church of England, for it was a very high Church and much more in keeping to that of the Brethren of my childhood.

I was focussed on my ambition to become a nurse and nothing was going to distract that from me. I was working and saving money.

Andy had joined the Navy at 17, with a desire to see the world, and he thought that this was the best way. As a child, primary schooling became difficult, for his Father was headmaster at Burleydam School, the school that Andy should have attended. It is not easy to attend a school where one of your parents is a teacher, let alone the Head master.

Andy in tropical whites

To make educational progress, Andy was sent to a private school in Whitchurch Shropshire, the White House, until eleven and then to

Sandbach School. In addition to his teaching post, his Father was Methodist Lay Preacher.

Andy was not happy in the Navy, his strict beliefs, ingrained from his Lay Preacher Father, did not coincide with the raucous life of sailors away from home and eventually he began to buy himself out from his tenure.

It was a pity as he was seen as officer potential and could have risen through the ranks. He returned to England and finished his service at a base in Scotland.

When he was there, he would continue to write to me and became aware of my desire to move to England. He wanted us to make contact as soon as I arrived. This was not my plan; I was determined to take up my nurse training post in Huddersfield.

It took me two years of hard work to save enough money. I was twenty-three by the time I had saved enough to buy that ticket to London Gatwick. But I did it and with great trepidation, bought my ticket and made preparations for my departure.

This was to be a new adventure, a new chapter in my life, travelling to a foreign land, on an aeroplane for the first time. The size of the British Caledonian 707 sitting on the airport apron, shocked me. How will this get off the ground?

I was allocated a window seat and as the flight was not full, there was an empty seat between me and a man in the aisle seat. The flight attendants were very busy looking after us, with constant offers of alcoholic drinks. I did not take up their offers, for I didn't drink alcohol.

Having said no thank you several times, the man, a very rude man, turned to me and said,

"For goodness's sake accept a drink, and if you don't want it, I will have it."

I chose to ignore him; I was not happy with his attitude but fortunately the flight proceeded without further problems.

Arriving in England I had only eighteen pounds left in my purse. I was expecting to be met by a representative from the hospital which the Matron could have arranged. But during the two years saving the money, I had kept in correspondence with Andy.

Since he had returned to England, he was determined to collect me from the airport and bring me back to his parent's house in Whitchurch, Cheshire. He had made a special purchase of a car, a Mini Cooper to do that, and there he was when I exited the arrivals hall at Gatwick. He must have risen very early to be there, for my flight which had not been direct having to stop on the way, would have landed in the very early morning. Our meeting was not easy.

As a child I had read books about England, how green it was and the pictures of pure white sheep and cows had stayed in my memory. On the journey from Gatwick, the land was truly very green, much like the rainforest in my native home, but completely different to the dried-up lands of most of the Malaya that I knew. There were no motorway connections in 1972, so the journey took a long time. I was able to appreciate the country side and was very impressed by the black and white cows.

Andy and the Mini Cooper in
Scotland

On arrival in Low Manesty,
Whitchurch, late in the afternoon, I
was welcomed by the family, his
parents, brothers and sisters. The
family atmosphere was overwhelming

and I felt that loving atmosphere immediately.

When I had recovered from my travelling, Andy wanted to take me out and show me Cheshire. I had come from a very hot country and was not fully equipped for the climate change with the clothes I had brought with me. I purchased a blue jacket, a type of anorak you could call it. Andy took me to Beeston Castle.

Beeston Castle is one of the most dramatic ruins in the English landscape. Built by the Earl of Chester, in the 1220s, the castle incorporated the banks and ditches of an Iron Age hillfort. It was demolished during the English Civil War.

As you can imagine being part of an old hill fort it was a considerable climb to the top. As we climbed it began to rain, torrential rain and I got soaked through. So much so that the blue die from my new coat ran out and I returned to Ightfield a nice blue colour all over.

Andy's mother was very cross with him for subjecting me to that. The climate change, the soaking I received and the cold shivering return to the house, laid me low for a few days which I spent in bed in a room I shared with Andy's sister.

That room had given me my first shock to my childhood memories in the books I had read, for waking up after my first night there, I looked out of the window and there were sheep. Not pure white sheep of my childhood books, but ragged dirty sheep.

The gardens of the family house only held apple and pear trees, so different to the range of exotic fruits that I was used to. At the orphanage we had Mango, Banana, Star fruit and coconut trees. As children we would use long hooked sticks to pull the branches down and collect the fruit before the birds and insects devoured them.

The coconut trees were climbed by the gardener who would cut the coconuts down for us to drink the coconut milk. In a way, compared to Burleydam it was paradise. I suppose in that way we were fortunate as children.

I stayed in Ightfield until my place in the nurses' home in Huddersfield was assured and I had recovered from rain soaking. I was soon to begin my nursing career in Yorkshire.

When back in Ightfield off duty, Andy and I joined a youth group called Unity 8 in Whitchurch the group was literally like a Christian Youth Group. The only time I remember feeling very at ease and in the right place was when the Church to which the group belonged, decided to organize a weekend or a week's holiday.

Camping in France, it was one which was very Brethren like, where we got up each morning, had prayers followed by Bible study, then we could go to the seaside have fun. Each evening we had Bible study again, and it was a very organized Bible Camp weekend.

When I was dismissed by Miss Phyllis, I was free because I left the mission, but very unhappily I left her, for I had been a Brethren believer up to that time.

I took myself away. I didn't go back to the brand-new Brethren Church. I went to Church of England and then when I met Andy, he was in the Freeway Angelical Church, which I felt was very lively and very different from ours, for the movement is very free. Ladies would speak in the Congregation and it wasn't restricted like the Brethren to which I compared it.

The Church of England I quite preferred. The quiet way they held their service. It was a very high Church, the next best thing for me coming from the Brethren background.

A Qualified Nurse

In England, I worked in Huddersfield in a Geriatric ward becoming one of the ward Sisters favourites, much to the disdain of the other nurses. I worshiped in the hospital chapel and I took breaks to do that. My interaction with the Ward Sister gave me the ability to do that. I asked the patients if they would like to go with me. They agreed and with the consent of the Sister, she was pleased for them to do so, but it didn't turn good with the other nurses at all.

Nobody else wanted to help me take the patients to Chapel. On Sundays I expressed my desire to worship, and although we were allowed breaks, it would not be long enough. I asked the Sister if I could extend my time by taking some of the patients with me. She agreed to let me do that. I don't think the other nurses wanted to do it, but they didn't like the idea that the sister said to me, "when you go with the patients that can be your break time".

She told me that when I came back from Chapel, I should go to her office to have a coffee with her. And I did it once and I never did it again because I was sneered at and literally put through abuse by the other nurses.

At first, I didn't fully realise the consequences that would occur. I took some of the patients with me and wheeled to and from the chapel for Sunday service. Unfortunately, it didn't go down well with the other nurses. They began to gang up on me, calling me all sorts of names. When I had to do beds with any of them, they would pull the sheets off me and mock me. I felt very uncomfortable.

I didn't attend the services for a while until the sister in charge realised that I hadn't asked to go again. In the end I had to tell her the reason. She insisted that I carried on and to take the patients with me. Life was strange! One can never be too kind, or do one's best! Somehow, someone, somewhere will always try and find fault with you.

The jealousy became obvious when I was making a bed with another nurse, the traditional hospital corner folding at the foot end. I had completed my side but she hadn't. Much to my surprise she gave a huge tug on the sheet to deliberately unfold my completed corner. I could see the dislike in her face.

I have learnt to manage people's behaviour and forgive those who misunderstand my directions in life. Even now, I continue to be on my guard as to why and which people might misunderstand.

Working in that Geriatric ward was a shock to my held beliefs on treating the elderly. Confucius, the renowned Chinese philosopher and politician of the Spring and Autumn period. emphasized personal and governmental morality, correctness of social relationships, justice and sincerity

In China, placing your parents in retirement homes - hospitals would see you labelled as uncaring child. To abandon one's family is considered deeply dishonourable. Even in extreme circumstances, there seems to be little deviation from this belief. When tackling such degenerative illnesses as Alzheimer's disease, most families would prefer hiring a permanent caregiver than to place their relative in a nursing home or hospital ward.

Western societies have become increasingly uncomfortable with the view that retirement is the end of one's useful contribution to society. In Chinese society, however, taking care of one's parents is the lot of all children – failure to do so would mean a major loss of face for any family. From all sections of society, children receive consistent reminders that they owe everything to their parents and that they must repay this debt in full.

I wonder now, looking back, if this was the beginning of my thoughts towards my future volunteer work, for my efforts have certainly been directed to helping the ageing population. The Chinese culture being spread amongst the local population of Cheshire by someone, who from early beginnings, was Chinese who is not Chinese!

I was to be in training for two years and before qualification worked in the hospital in Huddersfield, living in the nurses' home. We had strict rules about men being allowed into the building which I strictly obeyed as I did not want to upset the Matron who had given me the job. I was given the responsibility as a monitor of these rules. We all accepted this ruling for it was meant mainly as security for us all.

At Huddersfield, I was the only Chinese nurse in the hospital. As such

I stood out from the remaining nurses and to an extent, it was a little culture shock, but I was ready to do my very best.

I would sit in my room on my day off, or maybe Andy would come and pick me up and take me to his home. When I was studying, I could hear the Irish girls talking loudly getting ready to go out, as soon as their day sessions were over.

I made the mistake of telling them it was my birthday and they decided to take me out. Because I was the monitor of the whole nursing home, they were very aware that if they did anything wrong, I would have to report the case. To avoid this, they wanted to take me out and I refused.

When I came back to my room, as I came off duty, they took the key off me and showed me the shower; told me to get dressed. They got a taxi and took me out and I'll never forget how wrong that was. They took me out when it was late, which I could not understand. Why did they go out at 11 o'clock at night when they could take advantage of a meal between 5 o'clock and eight o'clock? I was told that the entertainment doesn't start until late.

I had no idea. I'd never been before, so they took me to a place, I think was a pub. I would have called it a dungeon. It was a huge house. I don't know where it was, I don't remember but I was shocked and because I was tired, I wasn't happy.

I wanted to be in bed at that time. I didn't want to go out at that time. They took me to this place and somebody said what would you like to drink?

Obviously, I never drank in my life, all I wanted was just a Coke which they got for me. When I drank that coke, I felt something wasn't right in that drink. As soon as they looked away, I found a flower pot somewhere and poured it away. I believe the drink was spiked.

I sat there with another girl, Sheila. She was a decent girl I remember clearly. I was determined to go home, I'm going home. I'm not staying anymore. They said you can't go home. It's too far as well, whatever you do not try to get home, for we are staying for a bit longer. We stayed together I stuck with Sheila.

The whole place was badly lit I said to Sheila, I don't like this place, I'm going; I took my handbag. I'm going to see where and how I can get back to the nurse's home. Sheila said she wanted to get too, so we decided to look for help and get a taxi back to the nurse's home.

I wanted to go to the toilet, she told me that it was upstairs. To my horror there were rooms everywhere upstairs, the Irish girls were all on the floor. At the time I didn't know what they were doing. The rooms were filled with smoke. I came downstairs, I said I'm going, that's it enough for me.

I can clearly remember that they were very cross with me but before the month is out, and as we got paid at the end of the month, these girls were absolutely broke.

They used to come and borrow money off me and said they had to have money for food, so I lent them some once or twice.

I usually said

"Please can I have my money back?"

 They said,

"We can't repay you, we haven't got any money".

When the next month came, they asked me to lend them some more. It used to go on and on, me lending the money until I told Andy.

Andy, who was now running down the final months of his Naval Service, was based in Scotland, Rosyth. 262 miles away from Huddersfield, it would take about five hours to drive from there. When he had time off, he would make the journey to see me.

In the week, he would telephone, but the only call box was on the ground floor and I was on the second floor. People would take the call and shout up to me. Many a time I told them to let it go.

With the strict rules of male entry, if Andy came, he could not come in. To let me know he was there, he would throw stones at my window to tell me he was outside.

On one occasion, in a very cold winter he came and I didn't want to see him. When the stones hit my window, I ignored them. Getting up for work the next day, his car was still there. He must have slept in it. Whether he had brought blankets and food with him I do not know. When he saw me leaving for work, he got out of the car and all he could say was

"When do you finish!"

And waited for me to come off duty and took me out.

After that I did spend some of my weekends off in Ightfield with his parents, Rodnight and Alma, for I liked the family atmosphere there. I had been welcomed by all, being accepted into a Family home, was something new to me.

After graduating, I decided to come to live with Andy's parents and under their influence. I came to Whitchurch to work in the Cottage Hospital, for a year. I didn't actually work in the hospital in Huddersfield post-training.

I had always liked the idea of becoming an Orthopaedic Nurse. During that first-year post Huddersfield, I decided it would be good to take further training. I offered to take extra training as an orthopaedic nurse, working in the specialist hospital, the Robert Jones and Agnes Hunt orthopaedic hospital in Oswestry, having gained that qualification, I used it for a while but I needed a change and decided to be a district nurse. It was almost as though I was searching for the right calling.

I was able to obtain a transfer to the specialist Orthopaedic Hospital in Oswestry, Shropshire, living in the nurse's quarters there. This wasn't too far from Andy's home so our relationship continued to build. I enjoyed working in the wards at Oswestry, spending my days off back in Whitchurch, with Andy.

Having obtained my qualifications in orthopaedics, I took a post as a district nurse in Cheshire to be close to Andy, who was based in Runcorn.

I did quite frequent changes; I just wanted extra training. When I moved to Widnes, to be near Andy who had a teaching job in Runcorn, I rented a nurse's house there and I would remain for another year or two.

My life was sort of based on work and the church not as much. At the weekend when I was off, I would come back and join Andy with the youth club, he was a member there.

When Andy picked me up from Gatwick, I felt he was just a friend. There was nothing much in it. But experience with his parents did sort of open my eyes to how a family life should be because it was quite a special relationship which they had.

I had never seen a loving father with a loving wife, with the loving children in the context of a local Christian home.

I remember cooking the first Chinese meal for my parents-in-law. And I did a stir-fry Chow Mein and they were horrified. What I was cooking, was new to them, because they were so traditional, Sunday Roast each Sunday and cottage pie on Wednesday.

They had a cleaner who came on a Wednesday. Each time she came we had a mince-meat dinner made for her.

Then on a Sunday afternoon after a Church morning service we had a traditional lunch and after that, probably before we went to the evening service, we would sit by the fire. They had some open fires then. Andy's mother had a coffee percolator that used to plug in. My mother-in-law would make the milky coffee and just plug it in and we sat by the fire and had some cucumber sandwiches for afternoon tea.

I thought it was so English, so lovely. I used to have cucumber sandwiches when I was in Malaysia and it just made sense. Afternoon tea, and I still think of it when I have cucumbers. I would often do it for myself because that's how I was brought up.

Being part of the Christian Youth group was something I had not experienced before. I am sure that this helped to reorganise my relationship with Andy. When his Naval career ended, he returned home he took up a teacher training course at Alsager

College.   On graduation he took a teaching post in Runcorn.

Chapel

One day, Andy said to me

"I have bought you a house!"

He had never discussed this before, and I wondered where he had got the money from.   An aged Aunt had recently died and I believe he must have inherited a sum from her.

He offered to take me to see the Chapel and produced the key.   It was huge, reminiscent of the medieval locks you can see in a museum.   I wondered what on earth he had bought.

It was a dark, cold, wintry November evening when Andy and my future in-laws took me to view this chapel for sale. Down a long and overgrown path, we came to this old chapel.

The key that was given to me was long and rusty. I was truly amazed and wondered at the sight of it when the creaking door finally pushed open. It was a disused Methodist Church.

Broomhall and Sound Methodist Chapel in Newtown was founded in 1838 as Broomhall Church, it belonged successively to the Wesleyan Methodist Association, United Methodist Free Churches and United Methodist Church. It was built by Joseph Cartlidge. In 1973, it amalgamated with Sound Heath Chapel.

Work begins

As I pushed open the creaking door, I saw that the blue drapery, cob-webbed curtains still remained intact. The pews and hymn numbers were still in place. The piano still in tune. The Church furniture was still in place even the organ.

I did not know what to say, but Andy, had many ideas with what he could do with it.

'This is our future home'

He was insistent that we could restore this and make a pleasant family home.

It was a lot to take in. I thought for a while that I had left the Church back in Malaysia and the orphanage and now, I am faced with another Church!

What a task!

What an ambition to tackle such a huge project. I did not realise then, that from there on it was going to be just graft and hard work and faith to demolish and rebuild a home.

I did check with him that there no graves around the compound.

At this time, he was in training as a teacher and my wages would be supporting both of us until his qualification, so the restoration was going to be a slow progress. Only when and if funds were to be available

The pulpit stood proud, much as it did a decade ago. Wall plaques were hung with biblical readings, still capable of being read. The inside of the chapel smelt damp, crying out for someone to renovate, to revive the memories. I checked, there were no gravestones outside.

We started to demolish the chapel as soon as the sale went through. It took five long, hard laboured, painful years to complete. The project was carried on whilst we both continued our professions, coming to it at every possible weekend to work on it.

It happened in every season of the year. In the winter months, gloves, hats, scarves and warm clothing was worn to keep out the elements. In spring and summer, it was a delight to keep going.

We bought a huge caravan which initially was parked at the bottom of Andy's parents garden, but after our marriage we placed it at the bottom of our own garden. Living on site made working on the restoration much easier.

My job was to dress the bricks that Andy was removing so that they could be used again. The growing pile had to be constantly moved in areas away from the current activity. My hands were sore and raw. It was hard work but pain never kills and no pain, no gain, applied. We moved on each weekend, each month, each year and eventually it all paid off.

It has had its moments! Andy had many frights, falling off ladders, falling off platforms. I owe it to Andy for his patience and determination to fulfil his dream in building this project. His ability to cope and work so hard was incredible and his determination to do it in the very best way was exemplary.

To this day when I look back and see every effort that has gone into this home, it still amazes me. The hours, time, and sweat that built this home is just unbelievable. The front door stone to the original chapel has pride of place as a mantel piece in our dining room, above the fireplace.

On one occasion when I was chipping down a side of the wall, I found an old bottle, a time capsule, containing papers from the original build in 1875.

Two neatly folded Methodist preachers' plans. Lord's day plan, weekday plan and special services. There were preachers' names and post towns, revival meetings, tea meetings, circuit committees and special notices.

The extension

It was just amazing! Flower rotas and cleaning rotas and all printed by T & J.M. Johnson, Steam Printers of the Oat Market in Nantwich. An extension was finally built later to accommodate Andy's Father after his Mum passed on.

We called our home "Gilead", a quiet place to rest. I thought I wanted a name that came from the Bible. In the Old Testament, Gilead was a place where people could go and be restful and peaceful.

I found that the house gave me that. I thought that it would be just ideal for our house because the house was meant for anybody to come if they need it, because it had originally been a Church.

It's a home to our two daughters, Clara and Hannah who spent many childhood years living and loving the space and beyond. The country full of growth, trees galore, wild life and farm land. A place where one can sit and feel the presence of God. Beneath the fresh air, the space reminds me of God's abundance, grace and favour.

That building has proven to be a very good family home, in which we still live some 45 years later (2019). Although Andy has yet to complete the rendering of part of the outside wall.

At the time this is written, in the pandemic lockdown, God has granted the freedom, space and time to feel his presence near. To remind us of his everlasting, abiding peace and hope.

Marriage

The work on the house was progressing and had reached a stage where it was habitable. Andy was at work on the house all hours of the day whereas I only had my weekends off.

Aside from his teacher training Andy was attending a local youth group at the Methodist Church in Burleydam, a small village on the road to Nantwich from Whitchurch where my work was now based, as I had returned from the Cheshire, Widnes, posting. The group formed the centre of our social events with organised outings and even holidays abroad.

Andy proposed and I accepted and we scheduled or wedding for the 1st November 1975.

Wedding

Andy and I got married at St. Johns church in Whitchurch. It was a special day because Miss Phyllis Wilson, Grace and Sally (a former orphan), came to the wedding. Although I had not spoken much nor seen Phyllis for many years, it was an emotional day for me in realising she had flown from Malaysia to attend our union.

Phyllis and Me at the Wedding

A special day to behold as the witnesses signed the register and marriage certificates were issued. During the wedding breakfast meal, I presented my bouquet of flowers to her in appreciation of the love and dedication she had shown me in my upbringing. Little had I realised how much of her life she had given to us at the orphanage; moulding us to be faithful and Christian children of God.

It had been years of misunderstanding and worries and tears. When I finally left for England in 1972, to start my nursing career, I went to visit Phyllis for the last time to let her know of my intentions in leaving the country. I felt a sense of the unjust for Phyllis did not want me to go.

She remarked that of all the children that she had looked after, she felt that I was the one who might stay behind and look after her. I blessed her and wished I could.

I was able to re-connect with Phyliss Wilson again. It was a rather special and emotional time as we had not spoken since I left for the UK.

We, from then on, began to reform our relationship. Phyliss came to stay with us several times and with consolation, we connected and opened up to each other more and more.

When she retired, she returned to New Zealand where she became ill and frail. She passed away in 1982? In Christchurch on the South Island.

A lady who gave her life, her all, her hopes and dreams to orphans like me. I thank God for Phyliss and all she hoped for me in my future happiness.

Life Decisions

After we were married, Andy and I had decided that until the house was in such a condition that we could live in it, we would not have any children. I would have children after he had finished the house. That was the decision we made; it was a decision that it had to be completed before we have a family.

Children

Our first child Clara-Novello was born in April 1982 and was joined by her sister in November 1984. She was to be called Hannah Georgina.

Between the two births I still worked. I had a Nanny who looked after Clara, as I still carried on part time District nursing.

After Hannah was born, I was taken very ill. I had not recovered from the birth and was bleeding profusely. The week before I took for the worse, I felt my entire body was not right. I feared for my children, a baby at two years old and a new born.

I was visited by my health visitor. I explained to her my fears and immediately she rang the doctor and before long I was rushed into hospital. My health was deteriorating. I was admitted to a side ward where I got first class nursing care.

All I can remember was several consultants at the base of my bed, as I floated in and out of consciousness. I did remember people sponging me down to reduce my temperature or the injections of anti-biotics. I only realised what happened when I came back to consciousness that I had been placed in a ward behind the sister's desk.

My family finally came to visit me but found an empty side room. It did concern them and was soon told that they had moved me nearer the sister for observation. I feel so fortunate to be alive to this day.

I was taken to theatre and operated on; the rest is history. I spent a further month in hospital until my temperature lowered and subsided. I was able to have my baby in hospital with me and Hannah grew too big within that month to be kept in the nursery in the unit, so they delivered a bigger cot for her so she could be beside me.

My parents-in-law were wonderful. They took on the care of my household and cared for Clara at two years old and Andy.

After a month in hospital, the consultant told me I was lucky to be alive. Thank goodness for medical intervention.

I was discharged but was not allowed to lift or do much. I spent my re-cooperation in Welshpool with my parents-in-law.

I thank them for their love and care, nursing me to better health. I was surprised that my mother-in-law taught me how to knit. Truthfully, I cannot remember whether I finally finished that article.

I was and am always grateful to Andy's family for accepting me as one of their own, although along that road there were ups and downs. These were to be expected as culturally we were different in the aspects of our thinking.

It was our Christian Faith that brought us together. When I entered into Methodism, it was a joy for me to know that, worlds apart, we did sing from the same hymn sheets.

This setback took an awful lot out of me. When I had my final meeting with the consultant, he adamantly told me that I couldn't have any more children and I was very lucky to be alive. I owe my well-being to the health visitor, Jackie, who realised my demise and the hospital ward staff for the nursing care that they provided and I received.

Andy and me in Welshpool

To look forward into my life, I had to find a new direction. My nursing career had given me much strength. I found a great deal of positivity as I began to listen and learn from people I met along my journey in life.

Whilst lying there, recovering in Welshpool, I had much time to think and I remember it would be Hannah that used to cry when I left for work, which upset me, troubled me because I had left them.

I felt that I was treating my children very much like I had been treated myself, in a way abandoning them, I know to a much lesser degree, but I didn't want them to regret it.

When my children started growing up, I realised a lot of precious quality time was disappearing.

From then on, I spent an awful lot of my time dedicated to them because they not only went to school, they went to ballet school. As a child, I always wanted to join the school ballet classes. Unfortunately, that was not in my favour.

They performed and did very well. Many performances at the Lyceum theatre in Crewe, in the annual pantomimes.

Clara was chosen to perform with Bob Carolgees and Spit the Dog on stage. She received a payment when this shown on television. They developed the love of competition and won several awards and trophies. It gave me much joy watching them perform and winning.

They were introduced to a lot of things that now both Clara and Hannah still continue in their adult lives. Clara particularly now performs in dance and theatre for charity. She's in the group called Musical Mayhem where they performing in September (2019) in theatre, which is just a lot to do when running your own family.

I'm there every time babysitting while she's rehearsing and her children, my grandchildren are doing the same. The children's names are Elliot. Lucia and Poppy. I devoted my time to my daughters until they were in secondary school, that would have been 1992-93. I believe that they benefitted in a good way. They were treated in the way that made them think for themselves; I think it was for me in a way, to give them a sort of training them to be independent.

You can see examples of that by what they achieved, being able to help themselves, not just sufficient, self-sufficient. They always got jobs, doing different things.

Clara's children

Now that Hannah is married (March 2019), Benjamin has joined us.

When they went to University, I was proud of the fact that neither my husband nor myself, helped them in any way or any form to search for their University or direct them to wherever whatever they want to do in their lives.

I am very sure that they knew that we did this because of the way I was brought up, how I had to fight for everything myself. They respected that and both knew the directions they were going to go. Both of them sorted their own University places as well as acquiring their own grants.

We supported them through University and now they are in very good positions. Clara is a teacher and Hannah is a tax director.

I believe that the two girls have proved that you don't need your parents to support you in choosing right pathway, you can do it yourself. My joy is that they worked hard and made it by themselves.

Reflections

Looking back to the beginning of my childhood and now up to date, I realise that the orphanage created in me a very strong and independent personality. To say the least, it made me grow up very quickly as a child, having to learn to cope and mange my own destiny.

I had no parenting bond to turn to. I had to trust and rely on the missionaries to guide and protect me from the outside world. They gave me the very best in education and the religion or faith that I hold today.

The ability to be kind and understanding to humanity. To listen to others and have compassion for those in need, although at times I felt alone and despairing, I realised that over all my faults, that will hold me fast and that the life I lived in the past had given my mind to be more grateful, thankful, joyful and express gratitude to all those servants of God who gave their lives to travel to another country in the mission field.

To sacrifice their own comforts to care for children, less fortunate, in an undeveloped land and humid atmosphere, is surely to become an unsung hero of our times.

To all missionaries, all over the world, I thank God for their uncompromising belief in the knowledge that they were called to be servants of God. To comforts they lost. To heal the sick. To minister to unbelievers.

How would I do if I was to be called to another foreign country, to sacrifice my comfortable life here. To leave my family and friends. To live in an uncomfortable situation.

"Would I survive the journey?"

I doubt I could do it as selfishly. I feel I would miss all my home comforts.

Growing up in the orphanage I had to defend myself. No one was there to uphold me if I erred in anyway. No one to cuddle or love me at any time, especially when I felt lost and lonely.

The church and the missionaries taught me the word of God, the life and the resurrection. I still believe and uphold my faith in Christ until he comes to deliver us to his abode.

I have much to thank Phyllis and Elizabeth Wilson and many other missionaries I lived with. They gave me an insight into a British way of living. A way of life, a culture beyond my wildest dreams.

A life full of many blessings. I might not have known what life would have been for me if I was not found and brought to life.

"Where would I have been now? "

"Would I have been sold to a family and made a slave or used by unscrupulous people?"

Thank God, he spared me.

I lived with many other children, some older than me. They would have looked after me. I owe it to Grace, Christine and Wendy with whom I am still in contact. I felt they were my past and part of my growing up. We had fun playing with made up toys, collecting spiders in match boxes, games of throwing marbles to win bigger ones. Playing with smooth stones and chairs made up as though they were on train journeys.

We disagreed and disliked each other in many ways and yet we lived together and I never felt love for each other. I cannot remember being loved. I sat and felt a solitary soul, always wanting to know who I was, who I am, amongst all that was going on.

Life at school was vague. I did well and went to four different schools, all of my choice. I lived with different missionaries, never feeling involved in any of their lives. I was taken to school in a car and home again. Remotely on my own. Taught and tutored by missionaries.

Where did that get me, a rebellious, difficult, strong willed, almost a handful as a child?

 As I got older, I regreted my attitudes and my disappointments toward those that took me in. They wanted the best off me, the wanted me to do well in life. I was unable to please them!

However, I hope I will be able to appease those who have passed on in knowing I have turned the corner and that I have dedicated my life to those less fortunate, those who are lonely.

There are many scars in my life, many broken pieces that had to be mended. Many a song to be sung with joyous harmony. The scars are smoothed out, my life is free; my heart is unbroken.

 Life is good.

Christ healed me with his redeeming grace.

Once Lost

Now Found

Missionary

I decided then and I have thought about this for a long time. If ever I did want to go and give my life as a missionary, it would be to work in China. I say this because each of the missionaries I have met have shown me what they did, what they achieved and what they have given by their devotion.

I saw a television programme some years ago, and it was a film called the Dying Room. It was a very touching story, a real story, about the Chinese orphans being left in this Chinese orphanage where the parents had dumped them, the disabled, the blind. They didn't want them to grow up. They were all girls and they were left as not wanted in the family where boys were prized.

There is a particular scene, which I clearly remember, where they are sat on pots. I'm sure they would have filled the pots but all they did was rock backwards and forwards. There was nothing they could do.

What really upset me was towards the end of this film; there was a room where they were kept when they became ill. The final room was a dark room and that would be the dying room. It was terrible how they just left them there to die. I thought I would love to go there to give these children love and comfort.

That was the only time I sensed that if I ever wanted to be a missionary, that's where I would go. The Dying Room. It would have been a time that I could have committed myself to such a devotion. It would not be possible now.

Volunteer

I started my voluntary work, when the girls were at secondary school. They were well away looking out for themselves. I decided that I needed to get myself back to society.

The time I spent in the Geriatric ward at the Whitchurch Cottage Hospital encouraged me to work with the elderly and the plight of the patients in that geriatric ward in Huddersfield during my nurse training, had stirred me emotionally.

It wasn't nursing I missed, for I had had enough of that, it was the connection with people I missed.

I started working with the WRVS doing Meals on Wheels. Providing a service to those who found it difficult to cook for themselves.

When a new company took charge of this service, the Meals on Wheels, I was made redundant. It was very sad really because you know, there was different atmosphere for the clients with the new company. As a WRVS volunteer, you achieved more of a personal connection with the people you get to know with each delivery. I don't know what happened to the company that took it over.

In Nantwich, there was a service provided by the Gables Luncheon Club which did follow the loss of Meals on Wheels. It was set in a building in Beam Street called the Gables. The Gables has a long association with Nantwich residents and has been used as a community venue for over 50 years, providing lunches and housing various voluntary groups. As I was now free, I was asked if I would take over the running of the luncheon club at the Gables. I have been running it for about 30 years.

WOMEN'S ROYAL VOLUNTARY SERVICE

In the presence of Her Majesty The Queen

The Chairman, Lady Toulson, and Council of
Women's Royal Voluntary Service
request the pleasure of the company of

Mrs Judy Townsend

at a Garden Party to mark the Service's Diamond Anniversary
to be held in the grounds of Milton Hill House,
near Abingdon, Oxfordshire,
at midday on Friday 26th June 1998.

Please bring this invitation with you.

A building which stands in one of the main streets of Nantwich. A black and white building once used by many organisations, WRVS, the library, meals on wheels, lunch clubs and council meetings.

For many decades it has provided, via its Citizens Advice Bureau, much needed help and advice for folks of all denominations. Lately the Gables Lunch club, functioned as a meeting place for the citizens of Nantwich, whereby they can come in for friendships, trips out, Bingo and a two-course meal cooked by all the volunteers.

The meals are cooked twice a week with the rotation of two groups of volunteers. Tuesday and Thursday staffs dedicate their time and love to care for those who are lonely and unable to cook for themselves.

The club provides four to five trips a year. Outings mean a lot to the elderly who have no means of transport. The seaside resorts are their favourite and their gratitude is often expressed in the many thanks, happiness and laughter that can be heard on their journeys to and fro.

The Gables, Nantwich

The members are all very friendly and all try to communicate and uphold one another in times of need. Many members have found support and friendship, supporting one another in the times of illness. Throughout my time working at the club, I have found great hope and satisfaction in knowing the human kindness and forbearance in each other.

The staff are to be credited for their joy in preparing food for each meal. Pots and pots of carrots and vegetables are being chopped and mashed, whilst utensils are washed to the tenth degree. Preparation is paramount in the daily routine and cleaning, with food hygiene of the highest class.

Recent published research shows that being a charity worker is the happiest job that anyone can have. These people derive the most pleasure and satisfaction from their work.

This is yet more evidence, as if we needed it, that in society we have got our priorities wrong. Money, or the pursuit of it, doesn't make you happy.

People are happiest when they are helping and caring for others.

It is essential that I thank all the many volunteering staff who have worked over the years, cooking, preparing, serving and washing up. Providing for the citizens of Nantwich and visitors past and present.

May God truly bless and grant them much joy in knowing that they cared and loved others beyond and above.

Unfortunately, due this unprecedented Covid-19 pandemic, the club had to close and will only re-open when it is safe to do so. Many of the members are in those that are most vulnerable with their health conditions. Closure was paramount to protect their well-being.

I gave some time to the Lifeboat charity, the RNLI. I dedicate my time a lot to them trying to fundraise as much as I can, obviously because I feel the charity itself is very similar to how a child's being saved.

It plays a very important part in saving somebody from distress, from Death, from danger.

Lifeboat

The Lifeboat committee organise a very big event every year on the first weekend in September. It's such a wonderful event. It is run at a Marina in Coole Pilote. We have a lot of people go through the gates and we have raised quite a lot of money for the charity.

The RNLI is a very big part of my life's work.

Life's a Journey

Do not run through life so fast that you forget not only where you have been, but also where you are going.

Life is not a race,
But a journey to be savoured each
step of the way.

When I was approached by a friend as to whether I would give a talk to a women's prison, a few years ago, I was very excited. I had always wanted to work with the disadvantaged women in prison, to understand why and how they got themselves in such a dark place; to understand those who had lost their way in life. To get a grip on what had caused so much upheaval in their lives

When I was a teenager, I was taken often to a prison in Malaysia as a visitor by the missionaries with whom I lived. It was no surprise therefore, that I had intentions of working amongst prisoners. Our visits to those prisons were to conduct Christian

Services and humanitarian acts too. I remember sitting and listening to the Gospel being preached to the inmates.

When the day approached, that had been scheduled for the prison visit, I was, to say the least, apprehensive. As I drove to the prison, I did wonder what I would be confronted with. Taking deep breaths, I drove up to the gates of this enormous gated community.

A kindly and well-dressed gentleman met me at the gates and advised me to park my car right opposite the road on the opposite side of the building. I was asked not to have any mobile phone or any recording gadgets on me.

Doing as I was told, I parked my car and walked back to meet the officer in charge. I was escorted through two double, locked gates before I was checked and signed in.

Drake Hall prison in Staffordshire is a closed female prison both housing young and adult offenders. The building became a prison in the 1960's being used to house male inmates. It was changed to women's prison in 1974 and a semi-open women's prison in 2002. It contains fifteen residential units.

I had been invited to speak to 400 inmates. Two sessions in the day, before and after lunch. As I entered into the prison, I was given a quick walk around whilst being informed about the role of the prison.

All the officers were well dressed with truncheons and all the necessary gadgets necessary for emergencies, on them. The inmates were about and around us, some in groups, some alone. All were very well mannered and I felt quite at ease.

The entire compound was very clean and well-kept gardens were neat and tidy. Some inmates were gardening. An area was set for vegetables and chicken runs. Work details were set to clean the runs, collect eggs and vegetables, activity to the wellbeing of the inmates. Classes were available daily for the inmates in addition to the work detail.

There were workshops, a laundry, coffee shops, a gym, a library and a chapel (for all faiths). I felt that the prison was very well equipped for the well-being of both inmates and staff.

The prison officers all wore heavily laden bunches of keys. Every door, to every room we entered was locked and unlocked as I was taken to most of the units. The one that upset me the most was the unit that held those inmates in the age group 65 plus. They had single rooms but I noticed wheelchairs outside most doors and with a quick glance saw some of the older inmates sitting on their beds.

That sight was troubling my conscious. Why are they still there at their time of life? It was very sad and how long will they be residing in that place?

Such questions reminded me of how very fortunate I was and how if not for the dedication of the missionaries who cared for me, I could have put myself into that situation. I thanked God for my deliverance and thanked God for the missionaries who gave their lives for others who are less fortunate.

The morning session took me to a lunch break where I was escorted to the dining hall. It was quite overwhelming to say the least. The noise was very loud. The inmates queuing up to get their meals. Officers on duty everywhere, watching over the entire room. We sat and ate our lunch with plastic cutlery.

One of the inmates came over to sit by us, wanting to talk to me. An inmate I had met earlier in the morning session. At first, I thought she was a staff member, for she was very well dressed, but seemingly she told me why she was in and it became apparent, she wanted my help in finding her family. It reminded me of the old saying "never judge a book by its cover." I did not offer help. I didn't want to get involved.

The afternoon session was due and inmates were piling in slowly. When it was my turn to speak, I spoke of my life in the orphanage and how by the Grace of God I was upheld, given a new life through all the struggles I had as a child not knowing who I was and how it became a reality.

Life growing up amongst others was not full of laughter, nor was it easy. I needed to find myself. I was sent to live with different missionaries and it did not work for me. I felt so insecure and unhappy.

I ended my talk with questions and to my surprise, many inmates came forward to hug me and to thank me for my testimony and would like to be set free and do voluntary work as I was doing.

Eventually I ended the day, signed out, was checked out and I went to my car. I sat there for a few moments thinking of all the faces I had encountered. I prayed for their future well-being. The lasting memory was that some would never get out of prison. I was told that the atmosphere can be very volatile and an eruption by different gangs can occur at any time. So much of the officers on guard status was their own protection and that of other inmates.

Finally, I as shown a unit containing the most security. Here was held the rooms which contained the most dangerous inmates. I couldn't but wonder what these inmates could have done to deserve being locked up like this!

Justice and Peace

*Put peace into each other's hands
And like a treasure hold it,
protect it like a candle-flame,
with tenderness enfold it.*

*Put peace into each other's hands
with loving expectation;
be gentle in your words and ways,
in touch with God's creation.*

Put peace into each other's hands
like bread we break for sharing;
look people warmly in the eye;
our life is meant for caring.

As at Communion, shape your hands
into a waiting cradle;
the gift of Christ receive, revere,
United round the table.

Put Christ into each other's hands,
He is love's deepest measure;
in love make peace, give peace a
chance,
and share it like a treasure

Fred Kaan (1929-2009)

I feel great peace with my soul.

This is my favourite hymn.

Philosophy

One more step along the road would I go
From the old things to the new

Keep me travelling along with you
Its from the old I travel to the new

Round the corners of the world, I turn
More and more about the world I learn
And the new things that I see
You will be looking at, along with me

As I travel through the bad and the good
Keep me travelling the way I should
Where I see no way to go
Keep me travelling the way I know

Give me courage when the world is rough
Keep me loving though the world is tough
Leap and sing in all I do
Keep me travelling the way with you

Coming to the end, the final part of this book I should basically express my views on life, my philosophy and how that I have developed that in relation to a volunteer, life balance and how my faith that I developed as a child, has stayed the time now that I am in England.

I'm looking back, are there any regrets at all?

I think I chose the right options in fulfilling my ambition to be missionary, like the missionaries did who went abroad but my missionary work is in this field in where I live. I see my volunteer work, both with the R.N.L.I. and the lunch club, as a mission.

I've encountered an awful lot of different people, volunteering people, a lot of different people at church and that has rounded me up as a person immensely.

As for the after-life, I have no fears. I feel as a Christian, God holds the key to our lives. I feel great peace within my soul and the joy of living. In everything I do, I give thanks and praise.

It is possible to say that my life basically is living and helping. My personal life is quite small in relation to that. My faith has helped me in that and I'm happy in myself. I have fulfilled everything I wanted to do. I am peaceful and at ease; there is nothing that comes along that I can't manage; my personal life is not important anymore.

I look at my future?

The Gables is ready to move to another level and I hope to be part of its renaissance. It is very much in my mind at the moment. It could really mean that I have to change things.

I want to share with you an extract from a Japanese saying. It's about how in Japan when something is broken.

Kintsugi (金継ぎ, "golden joinery"), also known as Kintsukuroi (金繕い, "golden repair"), is the Japanese art of repairing broken pottery by mending the areas of breakage with lacquer dusted or mixed with powdered gold, silver, or platinum, a method similar to the maki-e technique. As a philosophy, it treats breakage and repair as part of the history of an object, rather than something to disguise.

When a bowl/cup/plate is broken in Japan, it is put back together with the cracks being filled with gold, creating a beautiful lining. This is to emphasise the beauty in what was once broken.

They believe when something has suffered damage and has a history, it makes it more beautiful. The same goes for human beings. Everything you have been through, everything that you are going through, doesn't make your life any uglier. Although it may seem that way when you are going through it.

It is up to us to choose to paint our struggles with gold and make them more beautiful. You are not broken beyond repair. You can pick yourself up and learn from what has happened, becoming a better person.

Because of struggles you have been through, you can wear your scars proudly as if to say – look what I have been through, it has made me what I am today. I can get through anything life puts in my way now. Nobody has a perfect life and nobody will.

It is up to us if we choose to paint our broken pieces gold and make it more beautiful.

You are broken beyond repair. You can pick yourself up and learn from what has happened becoming a better person.

Because of the struggles you have been through, you can wear your scars proudly, as if to say –

'Look what I have been through. It has made me the person I am today. I can get through any thing that life puts before me!'

Nobody has a perfect life and nobody ever will.

Don't be ashamed of what happened to you. Everything that has happened to you happened to you for a purpose. So, the more we deny, the more we complain and don't accept what has` happened to us, then it doesn't make it useful.

The moment we accept and find what is useful in our struggles, the things we have lived through – then just like painting the broken pieces with gold – turning something that could be ugly into something beautiful and inspiring,

When what you have been through is an inspiration for other people, then it was all worth it. So, don't get stuck on how things used to be. Every next level of your life will demand a new you; sometimes it takes being broken in order to become a new version of yourself.

There have been many scars in my life, many broken pieces that had to be mended. Many a song to be sung with joyous harmony. The scars are smoothed out, my life is free; my heart is unbroken.

Looking back to the beginning of my childhood and now up to date, I realise that the orphanage created in me a very strong and independent personality. It made me grow up very quickly, having to learn and manage on my own.

I had no parenting bond to turn to. I had to trust and rely on the Missionaries to guide and protect me from the outside world.

They provided me with the very best in education, religion and the faith which I hold today.

The ability to be kind, warm and understanding to humanity. To listen to others and have compassion for their needs.

Although at times, I felt alone and despairing, I realised that over all my faults it will hold me fast. The life, lived in the past, had given me a mind to be more grateful, more generous, more thankful and joyful, whilst expressing gratitude to all those servants of God who gave their lives to the mission field.

Life is good. Christ healed me with his redeeming grace.

Worth

Do not undermine your worth by comparing yourself with others.
It is because we are different that each of us is special.

Do not set your goals by what other people deem important.
Only you know what is best for you.

Do not take for granted the things closest to your heart.
Cling to them as you would your life, for without them, life is meaningless.

Do not let your years slip through your fingers by living in the past, nor in the future.
By living your life one day at a time, you live all the days of your life.

Do not give up when you still have something to give.
Nothing is really over until the moment you stop trying.

Do not be afraid not encounter risks,
It is by taking chances that we learn how to be brave.

Do not shut love out of your life by saying it is impossible to find.
The quickest way to receive love, is to give love; the fastest way to lose love is to hold it too tightly.

Do not dismiss your dreams,

To be without dreams is to be without hope; to be without hope is to be without purpose.

Do not run through life so fast that you forget not only where you have been, but also where you are going.

Life is not a race,
but a journey to be savoured each step of the way.

My future is with my Family

The day I arrived at Low Manesty, Whitchurch in 1972 was a day and time that changed my life completely.

The spring air overtook my senses. It was fresh and I could see steam coming out of my mouth each time I took a breath. I soon settled down to the climate change. At times my body felt and needed warmth.

Andy's family gave me an insight into family life. A life I never had. His parents were dedicated Christians and it was a comfort to know my Christian faith that had become evident and would uphold me throughout my new life ahead. They made me feel loved and I felt I belonged.

My family, Andy, my children, my grandchildren became a vital part of my well-being. They gave me a sense of belonging, love and trust. They are my only blood relations.

I brought up my two daughters with fear, not knowing how I was going to manage to cope. With no formal help, mother nature soon took hold and I had to learn the hard way.

I feel so privileged to be able to share and enjoy my journey with my family.

My grand children are my inspiration, my hopes, my joy, my smiles and my peace. It is all of them who taught me how to love again, unconditionally.

It is them who reminded me how very fortunate I was and am.

It is them who always remind me how they love me so very much, and they always say, their love extends to the moon and back. I love them all very dearly. How very gracious and wonderful that those little children can ooze so much love, so pure, so gentle and so forgiving.

May our good Lord always protect them from harm. May they grow up to be good, mindful, caring citizens who are able to uphold each and everyone in love and kindness, understanding all human kind.

There were times when I felt sad that I didn't have my own parents to go to for help and advice. Maybe a shoulder to cry on, but I owe it to two wonderful ladies, friends from the church, who took time and care to nurture me through many a situation.

Auntie Edith Chesters and Mother Mary Charlesworth were there for me whenever I needed advice when the children were ill. I only had to pick up the phone. They were heaven sent and my gratefulness for the lovely clothes that were brought for the girls on their birthdays and at Christmas.

Today, my greatest friend, Mary, is my sole companion. A lady of many smiles, generosity and inspiration, who like her mum, would be only a phone call away. An organist at our chapel where we belong. A gentle soul with a mind full of knowledge. I appreciate her love and friend ship. May God bless her always.

Epilogue

Finally, I shall pass through this world but once.

Any good therefore, I can do or any kindness that I can show to any human being, let me know.

Let me not deter or neglect it for I shall not pass this way again.

Stephen Grether

Acknowledgements

I have much to thank Phyliss and Elizabeth Wilson and for all the many Missionaries I met on my journey in life.

I lived with them my entire early life in Malaysia. They gave me an insight into a British way of life; a culture beyond my wildest dreams.

A Faith I depend on each day and a life full of blessings that I might not have known. What would my life have been had I not been found and brought to the orphanage?

Research by Wikipedia

Excerpts and Photographs from God of the Oasis, published in 2013 to celebrate 100 years of Elim Orphanage

Passages from Dust to Glory by Sim Sung from the Elim Library in Ipoh

And Last, my thanks to Rob Dunn for the compilation and editing of my thoughts over the two years it has taken to complete this book.